Love & Remembrance

A Journal for Bereaved Parents

By Margot Kenefick Burkle

Design by Janet Sieff, Centering Corporation
Butterfly photograph by Diane Robertson, Cape Code, MA

Thank you to The Compassionate Friends,
for permission to use excerpts from their book, **We Need Not Walk Alone.**

Thank you to Connie Mindell for your help with this journal,
for your support and encouragement during the most difficult times, and for your friendship.

ISBN:1-56123-104-5

Additional copies may be ordered from:

Centering Corporation
PO Box 4600
Omaha, NE 68104
Phone: 402-553-1200
Fax: 402-553-0507
Email: j1200@aol.com
Online catalog: www.centering.org

Printed in Canada

Kevin's Story

Kevin was born on May 27, 1997, at Yale New Haven Hospital and died two and one-half months later after a long struggle to overcome complications resulting from a congenital heart defect. With the exception of one night at home, Kevin's entire life was spent at the hospital, primarily in the Pediatric Intensive Care Unit. It was there that we spent our days and nights hoping, praying that he would pull through. There were brief moments when we thought he might. There were many more moments, days and weeks when we knew in our hearts that he would not.

Despite the fragility of Kevin's condition we were encouraged to be with our child, to hold and care for him throughout his hospitalization. The compassion and sensitivity of Kevin's nurses and physicians lessened our fears and let us be a family. The support and encouragement of his caregivers allowed our four year old daughter to be a big sister to her baby brother. For everything you did for Kevin, Kaitlin, us and our extended family, we thank you from the bottom of our hearts. You laughed with us and you cried with us and, most importantly, you let us know how much you cared. You are an inseparable part of our memories of our child. Our child is now gone, but we are left with wonderful memories of our beautiful baby boy.

Message to Families

This memory journal was written to give you a place to memorialize your child's life and death. In this journal you can share your thoughts and memories of your child. My hope is that this memory journal gives you a place to remember and share the special memories of your child with both friends and family. In working through this journal, I hope that you find comfort and peace.

Dedicated in loving memory to Kevin Paul Burkle –
You will always live on in our hearts

With Love,
Mommy and Daddy,
Kaitlin, Colleen, Christopher and Caroline

In Loving Memory

I want them to know we've lost something dear
I want them to know that our children were here

Betty Schreiber, TCF, Ashtabula, OH

Name:

Nicknames:

Date of birth:

Date of death:

Place of birth:

Place of death:

A Picture of You when You Were Born

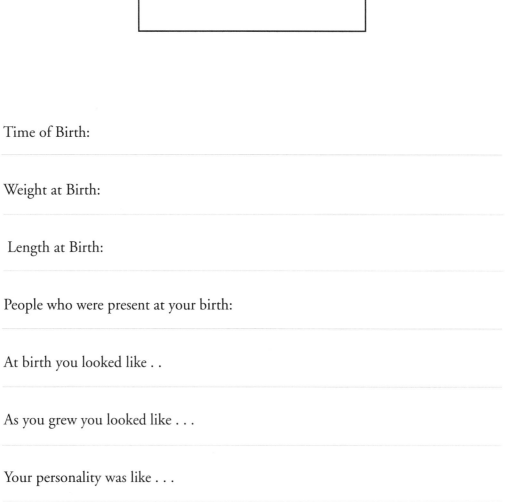

Time of Birth:

Weight at Birth:

Length at Birth:

People who were present at your birth:

At birth you looked like . .

As you grew you looked like . . .

Your personality was like . . .

"Firsts" in Your Life

Baths, Smiles, Birthday, Tooth, Day at School

Silently
While I slept
And the world went on
You changed my life
Forever

Alicia M. Sims, TCF, Albuquerque, NM

Your Footprints

As long as I live. . .

Your Handprints

. . . you too will live.

Photographs

How Fast You Grew!

Schools you attended: ....

....

Activities you were involved in: ....

....

Honors: ....

....

Close Friends: ....

....

Your hopes and dreams: ....

....

....

....

....

....

....

Sometimes love is for a moment
Sometimes love is for a lifetime
Sometimes a moment is a lifetime

Pamela S. Adams, TCF, Winnipeg, Canada

Family Portrait

Special Times with Family

Let the memories of the happy times warm your heart
And ease the pain while we're apart

Your Taste in Music Has Changed

When you were younger you listened to:

As you got older you listened to:

Favorite books:

Favorite games and toys:

Special Occasions & Holidays

Celebrating with Family & Friends

I know you'll never forget these happy memories of our special times together.

Milestones in Your Life

I think of what you were
And dream of what you might have been

Photographs

Thoughts of You from Mom

Mom and Dad please remember I am always with you
I am the beautiful white cloud in the deep blue sky

Thoughts of You from Dad

I am your own rainbow that shines after a summer rain storm
I am you child who loves you and thanks you for making me feel so special and loved

Dawn Callahan, in memory of her daughter, Katie

Photographs

Sibling Thoughts

My favorite memories:

The things we loved to do together:

The things I miss most:

The funniest memory:

Stories, Poetry or Artwork from Siblings

Memories & Reflections of Grandparents

Messages from Friends & Family

No Time for Goodbyes

How we learned of your death:

People who were with you at the time of your death:

What we were told about your death:

Messages from Your Caregivers

This is the hospital where you stayed: _____

These are the people who took care of you: _____

We know the heartache that you bear
We've felt the pain cause we've been there
We share a bond of infinite sorrow
A hope for peace -- Strength for tomorrow

TCF, Scranton, PA

People Who Came to See You
in the Hospital

Name:

Name:

Address:

Address:

Name:

Name:

Address:

Address:

Name:

Name:

Address:

Address:

Name:

Name:

Address:

Address:

Name:

Name:

Address:

Address:

Special People in Your Life

I have touched your life and you have touched mine, and for that we shall be forever grateful

A Special Service of Remembrance

Held in Your Memory

Date:

Location:

Burial:

Thoughts about the service:

Where there is pain, let there be softening.
Where there is bitterness, let there be acceptance.
Where there is silence, let there be communication.
Where there is loneliness, let there be friendships.
Where there is despair, let there be hope.

Ruth Eiseman, TCF, Louisville

Mementos from Your
Service of Remembrance

Music played:

Special readings, poems or words shared at your service:

Family & Friends Who Came to Remember You

Donations made in your memory:

Yearly Events in Your Memory

**Religious Services, Memorial Services, Family Traditions,
Candle Lighting Ceremonies, Memorial Garden**

*Now that you are gone
In your memory
I will carry on*

So Many Things Remind Me of You

You will always be the light that shines deep in my heart
I will always be a part of you and you will be a part of me

Dawn Callahan, in memory of her daughter, Katie

Photographs

Memories

I'd like the memory of me to be a happy one,

I'd like to leave an afterglow of smiles when day is done,

I'd like to leave an echo whispering softly down the ways,

Of happy times and laughing times and bright sunny days.

I'd like the tears of those who grieve, to dry before the sun

Of happy memories that I leave behind when day is done.

Author unknown